Letter to my Daughter Madeleine

...on the secrets she needs to know about men and marriage...

Adedayo Babalola

🌴 BOOKVINE®
publishability...

ISBN – 978-978-947-097-6

Published by
Bookvine (Vine Media Services)
14, Adeshina Street, Off Awolowo Way,
Ikeja, Lagos, Nigeria.
Tel: +234 803 806 9951, +234 805 569 6965
Email: submissions@bookvineng.com
Website: www.bookvineng.com

Dedication

I would love to dedicate this book to three people:

1. My mum, Mrs Olayinka Babalola, who I watched live out all the things I shared in this book as she lived in marriage to my dad for close to 35 years before she slept in the Lord.

2. To my darling wife, who is indeed my own "Madeleine". She has made life and ministry easier for me in a lot of ways; a Helper extraordinaire.

3. To my Daughter in the Faith, 'Madeleine Mwamini Kalibanda', who served me with all her heart for years, and told me she was getting married. This book is my gift to her as she goes into that new phase of life. The writings are the contents of her marriage counselling with me.

Preface

etter To My Daughter Madeleine is written to every Christian Lady who is married, about to go into marriage, or wants to be equipped with truths that she needs as she embarks on the life-long journey called Marriage. A father ought to be the first role model to his daughter but we live in a world where many fathers are absent; either through the rise of single mums, or fathers who are just too busy to be present. Every lady who will succeed in marriage and also enjoy it (and not endure it) must be instructed and taught. This will reduce the ever-increasing cases of divorce and many other unhealthy things we hear of in Christian marriages today.

Not just any kind of teaching or motivation will do, it has to be bible based and spirit-led to actually do the work. We live in an age where ladies are more excited about the wedding day and have never really thought about how married life will be. This is because the importance of a knowledgeable wife in the things of marriage has been silenced consciously or unconsciously. A woman should be prepared for marriage even before she meets a suitable man, as marriage is one of her primary functions in life; to be a suitable "help" to a man on an assignment.

"Letter to My Daughter Madeleine" is written as though by a father writing to his daughter who is far away, equipping her with truths as she starts the phase of life where a different man now plays a key role in her life. It has the appeal of a loving father writing from a heart of love and revealing truths to his daughter, truths that will make her enjoy marriage every step of the way, regardless of the challenges that are sure to come. Though it's a letter from a trusted man, 'Her Dad' a lot of what this Christian father will write will be backed up with scripture as he emphasises and puts Christ at the centre of everything.

'Madeleine' in this book is every Christian woman either married, about to marry or preparing for marriage someday. If you are a woman and you are reading this book at the moment, you are 'Madeleine'.

Content

Who You Are

My daughter Madeleine, I write to you, first because I love you and because it's my responsibility to take care of you and lead you aright. I don't want you to go through the troubled route many others like you have gone through. I want to spare you any hurt that may arise from being inadequately equipped for a journey like this. My dear, I ask that you embrace the truths I share here as they come from the heart of a loving father who wants to see you shine and succeed in life and marriage. Many of the truths I share here may be alien to you, but as you practice them in truth, you will reap the dividends of a beautiful marriage.

I also want to say that my desire is to give you all I know in this regard so that one day when you would have used these truths, you will be confident to share them with other ladies. As the Word of our master says in Titus 2:4, "These older women must train the younger women to love their husbands and to live wisely". I hope that one day you will be an example of the 'Older Women', a scarce thing in our days, who would teach the younger ones coming after them truths.

Above all, I will say to you my dear Madeleine, please remember that anything that would stand is one that has Jesus at the centre of it. Every life, business or institution that will endure the pressures that come with this world will have Christ as its centre. From him you draw love, strength, wisdom and all things that you need because in Christ you are complete.

The focus of my letter comes from Ephesians Chapter 5 but before I tell you what it says, I would like to emphasise some things. Do you know that the book of Ephesians has six chapters and that marriage as a topic comes up in the fifth chapter? This was strategically put there by God because He was trying to tell us that if we don't know exactly who we are in Christ and what Christ did for us on the cross, we can never understand marriage the way He wants us to, and therefore our enjoyment of it will be limited.

The first thing we need to talk about is WHO YOU ARE. Until you know who you are, you are not adequately prepared for marriage. It's not in marriage you are meant to discover 'who you are. Knowing who you are is what's going to help you function appropriately. Let's go on the journey of discovering who you are.

Who You Are

When I say 'who you are', I am not talking about your job, what you do, your hobbies and the kind of man you like. I am talking about who you are in Christ Jesus; I am referring to your identity. Identity is the first thing to know before direction and commitment in any particular endeavour. Your identity is not a product of your past achievements or future aspirations, your identity is the description of how our Master, Jesus, sees you. Before we dig into your identity, I must warn you never to let another tell you who you are, except they are re-emphasising what our master Jesus has said about you. You should not let circumstances define you either. Things that happen in your life and who you are, are two different things. Failing an exam does not make you a failure. The system and everyone around may define people by accomplishments, but you are who you are based on what the word says and this you must choose to believe regardless of what you experience.

A lot of ladies suffer from low self-esteem and insecurity because of things that have happened in their lives and what people have said to them and about them. They have believed this lies because they put other people's words before the words of our Master Jesus. This is a mistake you must not make. Many people feel unworthy today because society has set a standard of acceptance and they feel if they don't measure up to these standards, nothing good can come out of them. They believe you must look a certain way, talk a certain way, or dress a certain way, and everyone tries to meet up to these standards that are not expressed by the one whose opinion counts the most - God. Madeleine my dear, don't go that way.

You Are A Blessed Child

The first thing I would like you to know about your identity can be found in Ephesians 1:3: "All Praise to God, the father of Our Lord Jesus Christ, who has BLESSED US with every spiritual blessing in the heavenly realms BECAUSE WE ARE UNITED WITH CHRIST"

I want you to know that 'YOU ARE A BLESSED CHILD'. Never forget this. Your status as a blessed child is not because you did anything special, but because you were born of a Special God. You are not a cursed child, you are not a failure and you are not ugly. You are blessed and everywhere you go, you carry the blessing with you. The verse we are looking at says you are blessed because you are "united with Christ". Your relationship with Christ is what makes you a blessed child. This is something that must sink into you. You must never forget that you are a blessed child. The reason for the blessing is Jesus. You must realise that your presence in the life of a man is a blessing to that man. God has given you wisdom, abilities and skills that will help your man. This is why you are a gift to him. You are not a piece of trash that a man is trying to put together. You are chosen, ordained, and equipped to be a blessing to your man and this must stick in your mind. You are a blessing my dear Madeleine; this is why the word says that He who finds a wife has found a good thing and has obtained favour from the Lord. This must mean that you are a good thing and anyone who has you is blessed because Help has come his way. This is the mind-set you should have. I am not saying you are perfect in everything, no one is, but you can still be excited to know that you are a blessing - created and designed to help your man fulfil his purpose.

Beloved Of God

The next thing that must excite you is what Ephesians 1:4 says: "Even before He made the world, God loved us and chose us in Christ to be holy and without fault in his eyes".

This truth about your identity must excite you. The first thing we see here is that God loves you. You must never forget this crucial thought. God's love for you is unconditional. There are no conditions attached to it. God doesn't love you because you do well or don't do well. It is stable and does not grow, reduce or increase because it is already at its zenith - its highest point. My dear Madeleine, this is the truth. God will not love you tomorrow more or less than He does today, His love for you does not change. The love God has for you is at its highest point and will never decline (and it has nothing to do with what you do). This is why receiving God's love equips you to love your man and anybody else around the right way. Many people have a wrong impression of God. They think he is one angry fellow waiting for us to sin so He can break our heads and send us straight to hell. This is not true.

The Bible tells us in Romans 5:8 that .God demonstrated his love for us in that while we were yet sinners, Christ died for us."

God doesn't love you because you did something. When you were still a sinner and you couldn't do anything to save yourself, He sent Jesus into the world to die for you. If there is something you should know about God, it is what 1 John 4:8: says: "God is love". God's love for you is not based on how we feel, as you may wake up some days feeling like God doesn't love you anymore and is far away. What you are to do then my dear, is to get your feelings in agreement with the word. The word says "God loves you". The proof of God's love for you is not in what will happen but in what has happened. The proof of God's love for you is that He came into this sinful world and died for you, and not based on anything you did. This right there is love! It's in this love you must rest. This is the answer to any kind of insecurity that may arise. Be assured of the father's love for you.

You must ensure you personalise God's love for you as this is what will keep you going. By personalise, I mean you need to continuously bring it to your consciousness that God loves you radically because most times we forget this. A lot of ladies don't know this truth I am sharing with you, that's why they try to get love from things. This is the root of addiction. They want to be in relationships or even get married to get the love that only God gives. Many feed their need for love with destructive habits and while everybody else seems not to understand why a lady will act in certain ways, it all boils down to the issue of trying to get love from the wrong places. Many go from man to man ready to do anything no matter how wrong, just to ensure the man they love never leaves them; and when he does, they claim they were 'used', not actually knowing that they were the ones using the man. They tried to use the man to fill a void He cannot fill. They tried to get from a man something he cannot provide, God's Love. They force the man to be who he is not and heap unrealistic expectations on him. All these arise because they are trying to use the man to fill a void, a place that only God's love fills.

Perfect Love Casts Out Fear

It is only in Christ that you are complete. Any other idea is you putting unnecessary burden on a man or thing. Always remember that God loves you just as you are and wherever you are, and it has nothing to do with what you do. The beautiful thing such a realisation does for you is that it helps you live a fearless life. In 1 John 4:18, we are told that "There is no fear in love, but perfect love casts out fear". My dear Madeleine, God's love is perfect and it is the antidote to fear. A lot of women, and even men, have different fears and insecurities. It is refreshing to know that as you always ponder on the truth that you are loved of God outside what you do, it melts your fears away, whatever they may be. You are the beloved of God my dear, you are God's treasure. He loves you so unconditionally and it is crucial that you keep receiving love from him because unless you are open to receiving his love, you can't give love to others. I am sure you have heard the saying you can't give what you don't have." As you continually receive God's love, you become an outlet of love to people around you.

I have met many ladies who suffer from insecurity in relationships and even in marriage. They are always snooping around behind their husbands to check what he is doing, harassing him if he spends extra thirty minutes on his way back from work, always checking his phone when any text message comes in, monitoring him on social media to see who he is chatting with, and trying to read meanings into every innocent action. The truth is that the man in question is not always the problem, most times, the root cause is insecurity. She is not resting secure in God's love. Every man can only try but if you are not secure in God's love for you, it will flow and poison every relationship that you find yourself in. One of the terrible things a lot of women have unconsciously done through this attitude is to show their men that they don't trust them. It's not because they don't trust the man, but past experiences and not resting in God's love can drive a woman to unbelievable extremes. Consciously or unconsciously, it's either the man starts to fear her because he knows she is always snooping around, or he gets disgusted and becomes resentful towards her. Some men cannot just accommodate the fact that a woman does not trust them. This is why staying secure in God's love will make you rested enough to believe that God will lead you to the right person, keep that person, and equip you to satisfy him in every way.

Love Has No Reasons

The reason why I am emphasising on the Love of God is because the way God loves you unconditionally is the same may you are meant to love your spouse. The way you are accepted unconditionally by God is the same way you are to accept your man. Madeleine, your man will find a confidante in you if he comes to realise that you accept him unconditionally and love him without judging him. This can only happen as you love him with God's kind of Love. You must understand the difference between human love and God's kind of love. When people love you based on what you do, it is not pure, rather, it is attached to performance. There is the continuous burden of having 'to do' to keep the love going, but it's good news to know that someone loves us not based on what we do but based on his choice to love us. In this love, we find rest, peace and joy. That lover is Jesus.

Thank God for the many relationship seminars out there, but every relationship whose love tank is based on what a person does or does not do is not perfect love. The love we are to have in marriage and all other relationships ought to be the love that is like the one we received from God -*unconditional*. If two people give the unconditional love they have received from Jesus to each other and they love each other in that manner, then they have a godly relationship; a relationship based on the God kind of love. If you love your husband for a reason, it means that if the reason goes, your love goes with it. This makes it so easy for the devil to tamper with your marriage. All he has to do is to ensure that the reason why you love your husband does not endure and then all hell can break loose. Do you see why you are to love your man unconditionally? Your commitment to your man must not be based on what He does but on Jesus. If this is so, then you have chosen to build your relationship on a solid foundation. Your husband may change, will change, but God never changes. So if you base the love for your husband on Jesus, you are fixed. Madeleine, please remember that we are to love our spouses for no reason just as Christ loves us. This is the way our Master wants us to love.

Many ladies complain that their men don't really talk with them and express their emotions to them. The reason is that a man can only express his emotions to a 'spiritually mature' woman. Many ladies who are not matured in God's love have blown a lot of chances with their men. They do this by being judgemental. When a man tells them about his faults, failings and even fears (if he has any), a lot of ladies use this information recklessly to judge the man later when occasions arise. This is why instead of speaking to their spouses, they would rather not speak. When a man tells you about himself, treat it as top secret; comfort and assure him, never judge him. The truth is that a man will always be closely knotted to the one who knows things about him and does not judge him. They may never speak about it but this is the truth. Many have mismanaged information given to them in trust. Madeleine, don't go this way.

Sometimes, you may feel the heat of marriage, and the demands from everyone (family, spouse, workplace, goals and other things crying out for your attention) and you may feel exhausted. This is when you need to receive a fresh revelation of God's love. This is where you are to start meditating on God's love for you. This is when you start thanking him that he loves you so uniquely regardless of your wrongs, your failures and weaknesses. You will realise that you will start to experience a fresh supply of strength as you bask in the fresh glow of his love as revealed to you in the person of Jesus. Even though I am your earthly father, I love you but I have never taken time to count the hair on your head. God loves you so much He knows the number of strands on your head. He is concerned about the little things and the big things. Thinking this way will see you through days that seem long and hard.

I remember the story of a lady who was feeling really pressured on every side and was so anxious because she had been married for a couple of years and had not conceived a child. She was crushed by the silence of her husband, the expectations of her mother-in law and the never-ending questions of her friends and family members. The pressure seemed too much and she couldn't afford a smile. Happiness was far away until she was reminded of how much the father loved her and how Jesus came to die for her. She realised that if God gave her Jesus Christ the only begotten son, he would definitely give her all things. As she thought on these beautiful truths, she started to smile again and joy filled her life. Before long, she had a beautiful baby girl and everyone around rejoiced with her! Always remember, pressures may come, but you should stand strong through them remembering that God loves you.

Many will say to you "love your husband", which is correct, but the truth is you can't love your husband until you know how much God loves you. You are to keep reminding yourself that you are loved unconditionally, accepted and esteemed by God. If you don't remember this always, you will be building on a faulty foundation. It is as you remember and focus on the truth that you are loved by God that you are able to love selflessly as you have been loved, giving what you have received from God.

Love Keeps No Record Of Wrongs

Love is patient, kind, not jealous, not boastful, doesn't keep a record of wrongs, not irritable, ever enduring and ever-faithful. This is how the father loves you and of this that you have received, this is how you should love your husband too. May I remind you that "Love Doesn't Keep a Record of Wrongs" I thought to re-emphasise this because you need it. Infact, I believe everyone needs this. In the words of our master, *love covers a multitude of offenses*. Think about this, we offend our Master everyday but He doesn't use that as the basis of relating with us. We are not called to bring up things that happened last year, two years ago, or last week. Madeleine my daughter, just as God does with you, always keep the slate clean. Meditating on past wrongs generates wrong emotions which if acted upon can bring chaos. Bitterness is not something that just jumps on people, it is a function of meditating on the past wrongs of a person consciously and consistently. No house can experience peace if any party is always bringing up past wrongs. The reason is that bringing up past wrongs will put a strain on the relationship, bringing in condemnation to an otherwise beautiful relationship. We are all products of what we ponder on the most, and if a person chooses to ponder on only wrongs, even where the spouse has very strong positives, it is never considered.

Some people always use records of past wrongs to silence their spouse. It is important to understand that being tolerant is a fruit of the spirit and so also is the ability to forgive. Many ladies use the mistakes of years past to constantly flog their spouses, saying they are only trying to protect and guard him from repeating it. All they end up doing is straining a beautiful relationship. Always remember that those who are merciful in their dealings with others will also receive mercy from others and most importantly from God, but those who are always bringing up past deeds to silence and condemn their spouse will receive this as well. Madeleine, you must always remember that our Master calls us to forgive just the way He forgave us. He says to us that our sins and iniquities He will remember no more. This is the basis of the new covenant we have with God. If God deals with us based on all the wrongs that we do, we will not have the confidence to approach him, but today, we have access and boldness to approach him because of what Jesus has done. Just as we have received forgiveness from God, we also are to give it. It will be difficult for your heart to constantly receive forgiveness from God if you keep re-opening the sins of your spouse. We are called to give what we have received.

Love Is Patient

The issue of patience must also be emphasised!!! I am sure you would agree that our Master has been patient with you. You are not where you used to be, you keep getting better. Patience is key in any relationship. You must remember that you are not called to change a man, rather, you are called to help him. The changes will come as you take your place and prayerfully love him. The frustration of many is that they want to change a man, they want to forcefully get him to do things the way they like things to be done, which may even be the right way. No one can successfully change another human being. We are not called to play God. Play your role as wife and let God be God. One thing you must remember is that God is real and you are not Him. With faith and patience, we always obtain every worthy promise. If God has been and is still patient with you, it's only right you are patient with your spouse or anyone around you.

With regards to your man's family members, his mum especially, you must be different. Love her genuinely and let her see Jesus in you. Many ladies miss this idea, even Christian ladies. They bring in all manner of laws and restrictions into their marriage and they go on to talk about telling the world about God's love when they can't even love the people around them. I know many mothers-in law can be ……………………….. (fill in the gap) but regardless, always remember that you are also called to love them the way Christ loves you. It has nothing to do with what she does or how nasty you think she is. It's the same with your husband's friends. Wise women adopt their husband's friends as brothers; foolish women try to come in between her husband and his friends. It always pleases the heart of a man to see that his spouse is hospitable, friendly and not hostile to his friends. The truth is that as Christians, this is how we ought to be. The love of God dwells in our hearts and makes us attractive to the point where people want to be around us. I remember the story of a lady who got engaged to a man but ensured that she cut him off from all his friends just so that he would spend all the time with her.

Though, he did not say anything, the guy didn't like it. She ensured that whenever they came around, she put up attitudes that wouldn't make them want to visit anytime soon. This is not wisdom but foolishness. I am not saying that every friend of your spouse is a good person, but it is better you let your husband see your point, have a conviction, and reach a conclusion himself, rather than you trying to play God. My dear, always remember 'LOVE ALWAYS WINS'. No matter what the opposition is, love always wins. God's wisdom will lead you in all your ways I pray.

Holy And Faultless

Ephesians 1:4 not only says we are loved, it also says we are 'holy and without fault in his eyes'. The truth is that until you see yourself the way God sees you, you can't enjoy marriage or any other relationship. Madeleine my dear, it's important you come to believe that God sees you as 'Holy and faultless' in his sight. This does not mean you don't make mistakes, it only means that He has chosen to see you in a particular way. Holy and faultless. To be without blame or fault is the only way you can have a relationship with God. What God did because of His love for you was to send Jesus Christ as your substitute, to pay the price you owed for sin. Jesus came to earth and paid the price for your present, past, and future sins while you now have His life. So today, God sees you the same way He sees Jesus. He loves you the same way He loves Jesus. Your ability to realise and recognise this is what brings you into a place of relationship and friendship with God. You don't need to walk on egg shells around Him, you can just talk to Him and with even much more ease than you would talk to me. You may never have read about this, but Romans 5:10-11 (New Living Translation) says "For since our friendship with God was restored by the death of His Son while we were still sinners…We can now rejoice in our wonderful new relationship with God because our lord Jesus has made us friends of God."

These truths are so crucial you need to know them before you talk about getting married. If you don't know your identity, you would not know when you are being abused, when you are abusing yourself, or when you are abusing others. I have told you some things you must remember. You are Blessed, You are loved, you are holy, and you are faultless in God's sight. That's how He has chosen to see you.

Son Of God
The next thing you must always remember is that you are now a son of God. The scripture says in Ephesians 1:5 that he adopted us as His sons". You must always remember that God now sees you as his own child. You are not just a 'nobody', neither is your true identity connected to me your earthly father. You must remember that God the creator of the whole world is your heavenly father, and you are now His daughter. This should make you feel good. I believe you are getting an idea of how you should see yourself. You ought also to know that God is the King of kings, and if you are indeed his daughter, then that makes you royalty. It gives you a sense of worth and it would ensure you don't allow anyone treat you like a piece of trash.

Accepted In Love
Madeleine my dear, on the issue of identity, I would like to also say "You are accepted in the beloved". The issue of acceptance is a major issue and that's why I am bringing it up. We live in an age where people engage in all manner of things to gain acceptance. The media gives ladies an idea of what they need to do to be accepted. A good number of ladies don't believe they are good enough. They have a constant sense of unworthiness which is driven into them by the popular media. This idea makes them highly vulnerable, and they spend their lives trying to conform to an unrealistic image in order to fit in. Many ladies have heard people they hold in high esteem tell them things like *you are not good enough for certain roles*, and they actually believe this. Many ladies spend their lives feeling unworthy, bitter or struggling to prove a point because of this. In the midst of all

these, it is important for you to understand that God loves and accepts you. You are accepted by God and His is the only opinion that matters. God accepts you not because of anything you have done, but because of Jesus. You have no points to prove. Don't do things to prove a point to Him as He already accepts you in His love. The powerful thing about acceptance is that it gives you the positive energy to thrive; being all he has called you to be.

The pressure of acceptance has driven many to early graves and has made a lot of women end up with men who only pay them lip service, telling them what they want to hear so that they would feel good. I am sure it is good news to you to know that you are accepted by God because of Jesus. You don't need to try to compromise, lower your standards or try to fit in. You can be all that God has called you to be without any pressure or fear of not being accepted.
Madeleine, if you remember and let these truths sink in, the fruits of thinking right will begin to show up in your life and you will be at peace with yourself and others.

Forgiven And Forgotten

Finally, on knowing who you are, the last thing I would like to emphasise is the fact that you are forgiven. Ephesians 1:7 says "In whom we have redemption, the forgiveness of our sins according to the riches of his grace". It is important that you realise you are forgiven. I have seen first-hand what not understanding this truth can do to a woman. You may have made mistakes in the past, but one thing you must remember is that God does not deal with you based on your sins. In fact, the new covenant says "Your sins and iniquities I will remember no more" (Hebrews 8:12).

 Many feel so condemned because of mistakes they made in the past. No matter how terrible your sins may be, it is good news to know that you have been totally forgiven and God has totally forgotten about your sins. Sometimes, people find it hard to forgive themselves, but if God has forgiven you, then there is no reason why you should also not forgive yourself and move on. You must always remember that because you are in Christ Jesus there is no condemnation for you. Jesus went on the cross to take all the punishment for your sins (present, past, and future). Condemnation kills. It is the root cause of most sicknesses and diseases, and the reason for the large number of people who feel unworthy. Don't fall into the trap where you think that God is angry with you based on something you may have done. It is a trap of the devil. God has forgiven you for every misdeed; however, if you keep living in sin, you are opening the door for the devil to come into your life. This I know you don't want to do. You must also remember that if you don't realise that God has forgiven you absolutely and totally, it would be difficult for you to forgive others. This is why God tells us to forgive others as we have been forgiven (Ephesians 4:32). This is important as you go into marriage. You will need to forgive endlessly, just as you have been forgiven. If God forgave you all and is still forgiving you, it becomes easier for you to forgive others; husband, friends, children and colleagues. Forgiving as you have been forgiven is something you must always do.

Meditate on these truths I have shared with you, they must be things you never forget. You are blessed, blameless, and a son of God, accepted in God's sight and forgiven.

Now that you know who you are Madeleine, I believe it's time we talk about the main focus of this Letter: *'Madeleine the Helper'*

Madeleine The Helper

M adeleine my dear, the only way to be successful in anything is to first, understand it. You can't understand the role of a woman especially to her man unless we see what God calls her. In Genesis 2:18 (Amplified Bible), God says "It is not good...that man should be alone; I will make him a help meet (suitable, adapted and complementary) for him. It may seem like an unusual thought to you, but it is good that I state very clearly that the female gender, to which you belong, was created because man needed help. A helper is one who gives or provides what is necessary to accomplish a task or satisfy a need. It means that the primary function according to God's perfect plan for the creation of women is to be 'helpers' of men. This must indeed give you a sense of responsibility, but there is no need to feel burdened by this responsibility. You were built for it.

My dear daughter, always remember that you go into marriage as a helper, not as one that is broken and looking for completion. Your entry into marriage is not to create unrealistic expectations and dump it on a man. Remember, your primary assignment is helping, and that's why you are built the way you are. Always remember that being a helper is a position of influence and privilege. Everyone loves and appreciates those that help them but to be more specific, you must remember that you are not just a helper but you are a helper 'suitable' for him. This means that you are one tailored to him and his needs. Anybody can help, but suitable helpers are scarce. A suitable helper is one who helps the way the one who needs help needs to be helped.

You must remember that you are his helper and not his supervisor, dictator or mother. You are not there to tell him what to do and you were not created to make him feel that He doesn't know how to do things right. This is why you are a 'suitable' *helper*. You are designed and ordained to make his life better. This you can never accomplish by nagging or comparing him with others. Those who compare their man with another are not wise, but those who speak the truth in love are glowing with the wisdom of God.

My dear Madeleine, don't ever get the notion that things must always go your way. Someone once asked me why it is that men run off with their secretaries, I jokingly said "It's because God has created man to be attracted to those that help them suitably". This is not an excuse for immorality of any sort, but I hope you gleaned some wisdom from that statement. You will realise that the 'helper' is one who comes with subtle advice that are given as suggestions, they are willing to do what they are instructed to do. Most women start off this way, only to get married and think they have a right to enforce their opinions in the house in the name of 'women liberation'. You don't need 'liberation' because you were never bound. You are a help meet. It is at this point that the woman stops looking like a helper to the man, and other people fill the role. Always remember that a man will always focus unconsciously on the people that help him. He honours those who are above him, but seems to resist those he feels are trying to compete with him. A man may distance himself from anyone who He may be married to when she begins to act like she is competing with him for the post of leader in the marriage. Remember Madeleine, a man will always focus unconsciously on the lady who serves him and who he can discern has his best interest at heart.

Be Filled With The Spirit

One of the most important things you must understand in your role as a help meet is that you must be submissive to succeed. However, before we talk about submission, there are some foundational things that must be said. Most people talk about submission without talking about what precedes submission in Ephesians Chapter 5. Before submission was spoken about in Ephesians 5:22, verse 18 states: "Be filled with the Holy Spirit, SPEAKING to yourselves in psalms and hymns and spiritual songs, SINGING and making melody in your heart to the Lord; GIVING THANKS always for all things unto God and the father in the name of our Lord Jesus Christ." It was after this verse that submission came in. This simply means that it takes a spirit-filled person to submit to another person. This may be the reason why a lot of ladies try all that is in their power to submit, but never seem to be able to. This is one of the most important truths you must always keep in mind. This is because submission can be very difficult if you are not spirit-filled. Your flesh wants to do things the way it likes and doesn't like to do things other people's way.

Madeleine my daughter, it's only right that we look at how the word says we can be filled with the Spirit. It says speaking, singing, making melody and giving thanks to God, are ways to stay spirit-filled. This is very instructive and if followed, it will help you live a spirit-filled life. It means you should always have a song in your heart towards the Lord. It means that you must always regulate your life to live in an atmosphere of worship. Worship - praising and thanking God in Jesus' name, will always put your mind on Jesus, and this will lead to perfect peace in all areas. As you learn to worship, praise and give him thanks, you magnify the Lord. He becomes bigger in your eyes and things of this world become so small that they will lose the capacity to make you worry.

If you look very closely, you will realise that Spirit filled people are very easy to please and they don't always force their way or always want to have their way in everything. This is the God kind of life; always having a song in your heart and in your mouth. It is almost like bringing heaven to your vicinity and in heaven, we will be worshipping the Master constantly. It is out of a spirit-filled heart of worship and praise that you are called to submit. If you try to submit through any other method, you will struggle and miss it. Submission can be enjoyable as long as the person is spirit-filled!!!

Also my dear, being spirit-filled has many other benefits. It opens your eyes to many secret things. Besides that, every man loves a happy and joyful woman. Always note that it is not the responsibility of your husband to make you joyful. Your moods should not depend on him. Let the spring of your joy come from your relationship with God; who you are to him, and how He loves and adores you. A lot of women are like pendulums with their temperaments, swinging based on what people around them do. This is not you. Joy is a fruit of the spirit and you can exercise it. One good thing I know about joy is that it strengthens. The word of our Master says "The joy of the Lord is your strength", so anytime you are joyful, you are strong, and you make it impossible for the evil one to penetrate your mind and life.

Also, the word of our Master says "a merry heart doeth good like medicine but a broken spirit dries the bones". This also identifies with the fact that the happier you are, the healthier you will be. Don't let your happiness depend on anyone. They can add to it, but let the Lord and what he has done for you be the source of your joy and happiness. Remember my dear, EVERY MAN LOVES A HAPPY WOMAN. EVERY MAN!!!

What Submission Really Means

Now that you understand the foundation of submission we can go into submission and what it means. Ephesians 5:22 (Amplified Bible) says "Wives, be subject (be submissive and adapt yourselves) to your own husbands as (a service) to the Lord. The first thing I want you to notice is that to be submissive means to adapt yourself to your husband. 'To adapt' means to make suitable for a purpose, requirement or condition. It also means to adjust or modify fittingly to something. One thing I would like you to realise is the truth that you are called to adapt, adjust and be suitable to your husband. This is the instruction our master gives to 'wives'. Some women have it mixed up. They think the man is supposed to adjust and adapt to them. Though the Lord says submit to one another (Ephesians 5:21), he specifically mentions that the woman is to adapt to the man. Madeleine my dear, to change this order is to rebel against the truth and this may cause issues that are avoidable.

To adapt to a system will mean the great need to understand the system. It's the same with a man. You are to understand him, what he likes, how he likes what he likes, and how he likes things to be, and you are to do them that way. The thing about a man is that if things are not done the way he likes them, he will not notice or understand it regardless of the effort you put into that thing. For example, every man likes his woman dressed in a particular way. He may not force you to dress in that way, but you will realise that the day you dress the way He likes you to dress, you will get a compliment that he didn't have to 'plan' before giving. Yet, you may spend hours dressing in another way that please you and go unnoticed. If you want to catch him staring at you even while driving and noticing your new hair styles, do it the way he likes it.

The interesting thing is that our master didn't say you should adapt to your husband as a service to your husband. He says "Submit to your husband as a Service unto the Lord". Do you know that when you adapt to a man and do things the way He loves, you are actually rendering a service to God? This is one major truth that many ladies don't know. When they adapt and submit to a man, they think they are just doing it and because God said they should do it, but this is not so. You must remember that it is unto the Lord.

Another truth we see is in Ephesians 5 can be found in verse 24: "As the church is subject to Christ let wives also be subject in everything to their husbands". This is one of the most instructive things you need to understand, my dear Madeleine. You must look at the relationship between the Church and Christ to be able to understand the relationship between a man and a woman. You will realise that Christ loves the Church and gave Himself for her, making her holy and blameless; but the question is why are some people in the Church suffering despite the love and the provision Jesus has already given? It's because they don't know Him or understand His ways. This is why you should understand your man and his ways. Adapt yourself to Him, that's the way to enjoy all that marriage has to offer. Just as the Church submits to Christ in all things, this should also be your stand. Don't be afraid, that's God's wisdom. Know your place and stay there, that's where you will shine.

Every church that is suffering today is suffering not because God doesn't love them, but because they are not in submission to His word. As a result, they operate outside of His will and suffer the torment of the devil. It would interest you to know that Christ died for the whole world and the church is the group that has received the gospel. But even in the church, many don't enjoy the everyday walk in Christ. It's because they are not submitting to Him.

It's important that you realise that you are called to "Submit In All Things". Let me paint a clearer picture for you dear Madeleine. Have you ever seen a living church where they pray without the name of Jesus? Never! It can't happen, because the church is one with Christ. It is the same way in marriage. You have become one with your man and are to submit and adapt to him. This is why every lady must know the role of a wife before they sign up for marriage. God didn't say you should marry who you love, He said, "Love who you marry". This is because by the time you are married, there should be no more excuse.

I am sure you now realise why I said that a lady cannot submit to a man if she is not spirit-filled. It is only from that position that submission can flow easily. However, it is encouraging to believe that the one whom you are submitting to is not a monster who wants to take advantage of us, but someone who actually loves us as Christ loves the church. This on its own, will give you rest in submission.

Submission Plus

Madeleine my dear, if you want to succeed in marriage you will need to pay attention right here. I won't over-emphasise points but if I do, it's because I love you and want you to understand perfectly. The bottom line of every marriage is that you are to observe the marriage relationship between Christ and the Church. The more you understand that relationship, the more you will understand God original intent for marriage.

I would love you to see what Peter the apostle said to women concerning marriage. In I Peter 3:1 (Amplified Bible), he says, "In like manner, you married women, be submissive to your husbands (subordinate yourselves as being secondary to and dependent on them, and adapt yourselves to them), so that even if any do not obey the Word (of God), they may be won over not by discussion but by the (godly) lives of their wives". There are lots of things to pick from this scripture. He began by saying "In like manner", meaning he was telling women to do something that someone else did. So we need to go to I Peter 2 to understand what he was saying, and in I Peter 2:22-25, Peter was telling the church about How Jesus was submissive to God in coming to the world to die for our sins and though He paid the ultimate price for a sin He didn't commit, and ended up saving the world. Through His submission, many people have found their way to God, and in the same way (through spirit-filled submission), people get to experience a turn around.

Obviously, some people miss the point and try to marry unbelievers with the idea of purposely submitting to them. All I always say to them is that no matter who he is, he can't love you the way Christ loves the Church. This is because he doesn't have the capacity to love that way. A man can only give what he has. It's only when a man receives Jesus that he receives a new nature. If you have any friends who think this way, tell them what I have said in this letter. Marrying an unbeliever is a no-no, for your health and safety. God has some-one better! Going down such a lane leaves you hurt, however, if you are already married to an unbeliever, be of good cheer. The Lord is able to help you from where you are. The point I am trying to establish is that a woman's good behaviour in marriage has a way of softening her husband's heart even if he was hostile to her. The scripture I quoted above says "They may be won over". This means that if you are already married to a man and he doesn't know Jesus, through your behaviour He can get a foretaste of who Jesus is and then get saved over a period of time.

Madeleine, it's important that I emphasise this in case you have friends in this category. Many ladies want their husbands to know the Lord but they go about it the wrong way. They eventually end up turning such husbands away from the Lord rather than to the Lord. There is a way you can stuff the Bible and the things of God down someone's throat and the person ends up despising you and the Bible. They begin to hate having you around because you will only stuff more religion down their throats. People go to extremes of shouting during payer so that their spouses can hear their prayer points. They will play loud messages, disturbing their husbands and they never back down from always trying to force the person to go to church. If a man is not saved and would not listen to you and what you believe in, your love and life should draw him. These things should not be forced or else they would end up sadly.

The word of our Master says in 1 Peter 3:2 (Amplified Bible) that when they observe the pure and modest way in which you conduct yourselves, together with your reverence (for your husband; you are to feel for him all that reverence incudes: to respect, defer to, honour, esteem, appreciate, prize, and in human sense, to adore him, admire him, praise him, be devoted, deeply love and enjoy your husband). Madeleine my dear, I will always say that any woman that follows this particular scripture will enjoy the benefits of marriage. Also, like I stated earlier, it takes a spirit-filled lady to appreciate this and not rebel. I will look into a few of these attributes and try to define them so you will understand what they might mean in this context.

You are called to respect your husband. It is important that you see your husband as who H e is. He is your head, your master and leader. You must understand that you are not equal in the relationship. You are equal recipients of the grace of God - where there is no male or female - but when it comes to the marriage institution, God says he is the Head. Many ladies have never been taught some of these things and so they take it for granted. I have seen where ladies open their mouths and insult their husbands both publicly and privately. This is something you must never do. Remember that he is your head as Christ is the Head of the Church. Have you ever seen a situation where a group of believers (of Christ) gather to start insulting God or His Son Jesus? Regardless of whatever circumstances, you will never find this happening. Sometimes, it seems like God is silent and it seems like He is not present in a particular situation, but in His silence, you will never see true believers gather to insult Him. The reason is because they revere Him. God calls you to revere your husband as well. You must know categorically that it is a spiritual taboo to insult your husband in his presence or when he is not even there, regardless of whatever situation that may arise. Such should never be said concerning you my darling Madeleine. I am sure you are beginning to understand what it means to be married. To respect your husband is to have deep admiration for him.

The bible even counsels young men to remain single rather than marry a quarrelsome woman. It's interesting that the Bible says this, but it's because a quarrelsome woman cannot make a home or keep a relationship. She kills and strains it. Proverbs 25:24 says: "It's better to live alone in the corner of an attic than with a quarrelsome wife in a lovely home". This shows that God frowns at us being abusive and quarrelsome. Many ladies today wonder why they are not yet engaged or married. It's because many men are fulfilling this scripture. A quarrelsome wife will scatter any good home so marrying one is never a good idea. However, it must be said that being quarrelsome has a deeper root. Most times, it stems from a sense of condemnation, hurt, fear and many other negative feelings. This can only be healed by continuous mediation on How God loves us. To be a wife is a calling. It's a life assignment and one of your most important and rewarding assignments in life.

Respecting, honouring, and esteeming your man will earn you more than you will lose. The culture we live in today does not see the need for respect and you see people talk anyhow or act anyhow towards their husbands. This is why divorce is on the rise and some even think it's trendy to be divorced. Until we submit to the one who instituted marriage and follow the way He wants us to live, we may abuse marriage which is what a lot of people are doing today. I don't have a set of rules for you on what to do and what not to do as regards respecting your husband, but when a woman doesn't respect her husband, it is always very obvious. It is respect that makes you obey your husband's instructions even though they may not be always convenient. Finally, always remember that it is the level of honour and respect people discern that you give to your husband that they will also give to him. If you honour and esteem him among your friends, which you should, then that is exactly how they will see him. If they esteem him highly and you speak of him highly, they will regard you highly too.

Always show that you value and appreciate your husband. This is a powerful truth. This has a way of drawing him closer to you effortlessly. Don't be one to pull him down and always speak condemning words to him. Sometimes, your husband can draw strength from the words you speak to him. Little statements like *"I believe in you"*, *"You have what it takes to pull this off"*, *"I appreciate you"*, will go a long way when a man is stressed or trying to figure something out. Even when he misses it or makes a mistake, you can be so loving and supportive that He can regroup and refire as you encourage, support and appreciate him. Some ladies are the *I-told-you-so* kind. These are the ladies that say something and wait for their husbands to miss it so they can pounce on him. Please always remember that it is not a competition. Men don't get married so that the lady can spend her time proving a point or being right in all things. When it comes to the woman a man chooses to marry, he is looking for a helper. The word 'helper' is from the Hebrew word 'ezer', meaning to aid, support and give succour. Interestingly, it appears twenty one times in the Bible and apart from the places where the woman is called 'ezer', the other places this word is used is mostly in reference to God the almighty. This shows you that the woman is not just trying to bring him help, but she will also do anything to help him even when the man is down.

Madeleine my dear, praise, admire, enjoy, and love your husband. Praise does a good thing to anyone that is praised. Learn to enjoy your husband and his ways. Don't capitalise on his weaknesses, rather, celebrate his strengths. This is the way you can enjoy your husband because as you know, no one is perfect in his behaviour and life, not even you Madeleine.

I remember saying to you in the beginning of this letter that the word of the Master says "Older women are to teach younger women how to love their husbands". It will interest you to know that the root word of the word 'love' is not actually 'agape' - God's unconditional kind of love. The word 'love' is actually translated from the Greek word 'Philandros'. This Greek word 'philandros' was coined from two root words: 'Philos' - which means *actively fond and affectionate*, and the second word 'aner', which means man. The word 'Philandros' therefore means loving a man the way he loves to be loved or being affectionate towards a man in the way He likes it. This is quite clear Madeleine, and that's why it is important that I speak to you about 'Sex and Your Husband'.

Sex and Your Husband

Sex And Spirituality

I know you might feel awkward that I am writing to you about this, but we have to touch this topic Madeleine, and only because I love you. I have seen this issue cause a lot of problems especially in Christian circles. A lot of ladies never really have anyone to talk to them openly about this topic; however, I feel that whatever a person is not taught, there is a tendency for him/her to make unnecessary mistakes that could have been avoided had they been taught.

Sex in marriage is something people don't really like to talk about because it's perceived as a sacred topic. However, the ignorance on this issue is alarming, especially in the Christian circles. I will give you an example of what I am talking about. One day, a lady came to me and said that she doesn't have sex with her husband on Sundays because she is a member of her church choir, and sometimes she leads praise and worship. I was already wondering what that had to do with having sex with her husband, until she said, if she has sex with her husband before service, it will defile her. She was quite serious about this and I was really amazed. I couldn't believe that someone could be that ignorant on such an issue but the truth is you can't blame her. No one told her what holiness is. They made her believe righteousness is a function of what you do. (The fact that someone could think like this helps you understand the height of ignorance that is present among believers concerning marital relations. This ignorance is because they are expected to abstain before marriage and so they feel they can't open up or ask questions on this issue.)

I had to take time to tell her that a Christian is not righteous based on what they do but what Jesus did for us on the cross. He became sin for us, who knew no sin, that we might become the righteousness of God in Christ Jesus. I told her that it was not sleeping with her husband or the absence of it that made her holy or anointed or not to lead during Sunday service. Interestingly, she was amazed, especially after I showed her in the scriptures, and then she corrected her error. Her husband was so thankful to me and of course you should know the reason why. He had been the one suffering from her actions, and since he believed the same thing she believed, he just endured it, even though he was not pleased about it.

The truth is that when married believers are having sex, God is not looking away because it is not sin. Infact, God is there with them; Sex is a type of fellowship between a man and his wife and is not sinful in any way as long as it is within marriage. God is the one who invented sex and so He is not against it but He is pleased when it is done the right way. It must be said that when a man and a woman are having sex they are actually exercising their faith. They are doing the word. Faith is doing the word and if God says to married couples that they should have marital relations frequently, heeding to this is you acting in faith and this pleases God. Faith pleases God and if having sex is in the word, doing it is faith and it pleases God. I am writing this to change the perspective of sex that you may have as the world paints an idea of sex being a negative and secret act. This is only so because it has been abused and done outside the confines of marriage. Always remember Madeleine that sex in marriage is the will of God

Well, still on that point, contrary to her previous belief, it was when her husband demanded for sex and she refused him (because she was going to minister in the church choir) that she was in the wrong;

as she had rebelled against the word of our Master. One of the things I want to say is that as married couples, there is no time you cannot have sex. The only time you are told to refrain from sex is when you are fasting so that you may concentrate. In fact, the word says the moment you fast for a while, you should come back together in sexual relations so you are not tempted. I Corinthians 7:5 says "Do not refuse and deprive each other (of your marital rights), except perhaps by mutual consent for a time, so that you may devote yourselves unhindered to prayer. But afterwards resume marital relations, lest Satan tempt you to sin through your lack of restraint of sexual desire. This scripture is quite clear as to when not to have sex. However, there is a truth you must not neglect, it says even when you decide to go on a 'Sex Fast' (as I call it) because of prayer and fasting, it must be by mutual consent. This is very important and you must pay attention to it. The consent must be mutual and if any party does not agree to the sex fast, then it does not hold. Period.

It means if you decide to pray and fast concerning something and you don't want to have sex so as to concentrate, you must tender such a fast to your husband for approval. If he approves it and agrees to the 'Sex Fast' based on your reasons, then you can proceed with it. If he doesn't agree and you decide to starve him, then you are in the wrong. This, you must clearly understand. The same applies to him as well. If he wants to go into some days of fasting, he must submit this to you for approval, because it would mean you won't have sexual relations with him for a while and you have all the right to agree or refuse. Anything outside this is wrong.

Another thing we must emphasise is that sex (marital relations) between the two of you is a right that both of you have. A right is something that is yours. You don't need to beg for it or try to lobby for it, it is your right. In marriage, sex is your right Madeleine, and it is also the right of your husband. One thing you must recognise is that in marriage, your body belongs to your husband and his body belongs to you. In I Corinthians 7:3-4 "The husband should give to his wife her conjugal rights (goodwill, kindness and what is due her as his wife), and likewise the wife to her husband. For the wife does not have exclusive authority and control over her own body, but the husband has his rights; likewise also, the husband does not have exclusive authority and control over his body but the wife has her rights". This is very clear. You don't have exclusive rights over your body.

If all married folks understand and accept these simple truths, many things that occur in marriages would not even occur. As the wife, you must understand that your husband has a right over your body. It is not something you hoard or you try to get him to deserve. It is his right. Some ladies have a very unscriptural attitude of allowing their husbands have marital relations with them only when it seems like he deserves it. So they wait till he does something special. This is not only unscriptural, that lady is yielding control of her home to the devil. Madeleine, please don't go this way. Your husband has a right over your body so let him never feel like He has to do something to deserve it. He owns it and you own his body too. If you have friends who are married and they believe that their husbands should first earn it and they drive their husbands to do things just for sex, let them know they are not pleasing God this way.

Another important thing I need you to see from the issue of marital relations is that even after you go into a time of prayer and fasting, you are required to come back together and have marital relations. The reason for this is very important. Many people don't understand how they yield to the devil and they surrender their marriages to the devil, and this is one way they do it. The word says "but afterwards resume marital relations, lest Satan tempt you to sin through your lack of restraint of sexual desire". This scripture shows that a married couple can actually invite the devil into their home. People always say things like *"The Man Cheated" "The Woman Cheated", while some say,*

"It's the Devil". I agree totally with that last one because someone allowed him in. From the above scripture, we see that a person can allow the devil to tempt their spouse if they do not ensure they have marital relations to the satisfaction of each spouse. I always say that, all things being equal, *"a man will not eat outside if he is full inside*. This is not an excuse for infidelity, but you should not open your husband to the attacks and temptation of the devil. Think of it in terms of food. If you eat a lot at home, and you go visit a friend afterwards, no matter the kind of food they offer you, because you have been so filled at home, and you are not afraid that when you get home there might be no food, you won't be interested.

However, imagine you did not eat at home, and they offered you food that you love or even food that you don't really love, the temptation becomes greater. Madeleine, since we have established that your body is no longer exclusively yours once you get married but that of your husband, please do not hoard it from him. However, if for obvious reasons you cannot give him, please explain to him apologetically and ensure you don't wait till he asks again till you make it up to him. This is priority!

The book of Proverbs 5:18-19 says "Let your wife be a fountain of blessing for you. Rejoice in the wife of your youth. She is a loving deer and a graceful doe. Let her breasts satisfy you always. May you always be captivated by her love". Though this was addressed to the man, you can glean some wisdom from it. I am highlighting this because it is referring to 'marital relations'. The word says you are to be a fountain of blessing, making your husband rejoice. It also says your breasts are to "satisfy him always" emphasising that you are to ensure your husband is satisfied and continually captivated by your love. This is the way to ensure you shield him from external attacks.

Many ladies fight battles from the wrong side. You don't need to wait till you know that a lady finds your husband attractive before you start playing 'counter attack'. Your fulfilment is in giving your husband all of you; pleasing him and not going against the word. It is interesting how ladies will go against the word of God as it regards having marital relations with their husbands, and on that same bed they pray. How do you expect to follow the specific word when you have not followed the generic one?

Madeleine, Christianity is never a reason and will never be a reason to starve your husband. I heard a pathetic story of a woman who denied her husband sex because she decided to consecrate herself to the Lord for about a year. This is absolutely unscriptural and that lady opened her home to the devil as she has progressed in a way that is in rebellion with the word. All these acts of husbands asking for sex only to have the woman acting like she is praying is all unscriptural and carnal. It is zeal without knowledge that causes such acts and that's why I am writing to you. I have seen marriages go apart because of marital relations. Please be wise. Wisdom is always profitable and it directs.

You may want to ask "what are the boundaries in sex?" The boundaries in sex are the ones that you set, however, anything that goes outside the two of you is what is wrong. God has given two of you to one another. Use yourselves appropriately and as long as it's between the two of you and none of you finds it uncomfortable and inappropriate, it is fine.

Don't Be A Fraud

Finally, before you call someone a thief, see what the word says in 1 Corinthians 7:5 "Defraud ye not one another Do you know what the bible calls a person who refuses to give her body to her husband? The word calls the person a fraud. A fraud is a deliberate deception to secure unlawful gain. The word 'fraud' is traceable to the activities of the devil, so please ensure you don't go this way. Some ladies use sex as a tool of punishment, and even brag about it! When their husbands do things they don't like, instead of settling it amicably, they resort to using sex to punish their husbands. This attitude is wrong and you only can think this way because you have not come to understand that you don't have exclusive rights to your body.

I hope you will share this letter with many Christian ladies because they need to be informed. A lot of ladies take advantage of the fact that they know that God doesn't like divorce and God frowns at adultery. When their husbands do things they do not like instead of solving it amicably as Christians would do, they use sex to punish their husbands because they believe He cannot get it outside, after all he is a Christian. This is not only playing with fire, it is also a sin in that you are trying to make sin attractive to your spouse. Sex was not given to you by God to punish your husband or to use as a bargaining tool for your needs. It is a beautiful thing God gave you both to enjoy.

Sex is so vital in a marriage relationship that you can use it to actually determine the level of bonding between two people. It has been said that before a marriage crashes, their sex life must have crashed long before. You will always realise that a good marriage has a beautiful sex life. Madeleine, anytime you notice that the sex culture and frequency is reducing, it is a sign of something going wrong. When a couple first get married they seem to have a honeymoon period which most people say is one of the highest times of sexual intimacy. The reason is the two individuals are not expected to do anything or care for anything but bond. However, when they are now back to life's business, they get a rhythm that fits with their lifestyle. When this rhythm starts to reduce, couples ought to check it. Please note my dear, that it's not only a good sex life that makes a marriage successful, but it's a very important symptom that something may be going wrong.

Finally on the issue of marital relations, it is important that you discuss preferences, frequency and positions. These are some of the issues that a lot of Christians have been silent about and it has destroyed many homes. Many questions arise on issues like "One spouse likes to have sex every other day while the other likes to have sex once a week." I heard of a woman who said she didn't like having sex with her husband because she felt she could expand and get damaged due to 'over-use'. This bothers on ignorance. I must be quick to add that God will not have us do something that will lead to damage just by doing what he says. This is not an excuse for abstinence however when it comes to the issue of frequency, it is most times dependent on the parties involved and the sexual appetite they have. There are no laws on frequency but each party must be willing to compromise and have a middle ground for the sake of the other person. If the parties involved walk in love they will sort this issue out easily. The Bible says "Love puts the other first" so in the case where your spouse wants more than you are giving you should discuss it and reach a middle ground that is realistic.

Another issue that has caused problems as it relates to marital relations is "Sexual Positions". A lot of men have complained about women and also some women have complained about their men. Some people have ideas that they think is biblical but it is actually ignorance. I heard the case of a person who said 'Missionary Position' is the only approved biblical sexual position and anyone that tries out any other style is going to hell. This is very funny, to say the least. Nowhere in the bible did God approve or disapprove any position for sex. Whatever pleases the people involved is fine. However, it is important to be sensitive to your spouse as some sexual positions might be painful and uncomfortable for your spouse. Any style comfortable and pleasing to your spouse and you is fine.

Understanding each other is the most important thing when it comes to marital relations. Most of the time, a man is a go-getter and just wants to get the business done, while the woman wants to go slow. For perfect balance and harmony, it is important that you discuss preferences so that everyone is pleased, happy and satisfied. It's important to always remember that satisfaction of both parties is key and this should always be at the back of your mind Madeleine

Pre-marital Sex Can Be Avoided

A lot of Christian leaders spend time trying to ensure that two people courting don't fornicate before marriage, but it seems that after marriage, no one encourages ladies to ensure they satisfy their men. You may have some friends who are not married and they seem to be struggling with avoiding fornication. The solution to this is very simple. These ladies should just ensure they never spend time together in secluded places with the person they are courting. Many Christians make the mistake of thinking they have reached a particular spiritual height so they don't pay attention to the word anymore. The Bible says "flee all appearances of evil", and it also says "flee youthful lust". It's amazing how two Christians who are not yet married and are attracted to each other stay in the same room together these days. What they are doing is that they are trying to tempt themselves. As long as the two parties are attracted to each other, they are playing with fire and most times they get burnt. There seems to be a growing culture of people courting spending time in each other's houses alone. This is not healthy at all.

Some ladies try to deceive themselves into saying things like, "I am going to my fiancé's house overnight, we are going to have a prayer vigil alone." Sometimes, these things start innocently but if it goes on long enough, all manner of evil is conceived and before they know it, they get into wrong doings, get condemned, and start to justify the wrong doings. They end up with the cycle of sin-condemnation—repentance---and back to sin again until they end up searing their conscience and what used to look sinful to them becomes tolerable. A wise lady will ensure she doesn't leave this to chance. She can avoid this by taking someone along anytime she is going to her fiancé's place or not going there at all. Call it old fashioned, but what she is doing is that she is protecting herself.

I remember the story of a lady who was a very morally upright Christian. She went to a man's house alone and one thing led to another and they engaged in pre-marital sex. She spent years in self-condemnation, thinking she was evil for doing such a thing, but the truth is it only happened because she over-estimated herself and trusted in her flesh by not taking precaution. This is how people get into trouble. Madeleine, for your friends that may be going through this, tell them I said evil things like this never happen in the open. If they indeed want to stop such things, then they should avoid staying in secluded places alone with their fiancés.

This is just wisdom and people who live by it will enjoy all that God has for them. Another issue that could bring controversy in any marriage is the issue of money. So Madeleine, it is imperative that we talk about 'Your Man and Money'.

Your Man and Money

Avoid The Pressure

Money is one issue that I must write to you about my dear Madeleine, for obvious reasons. The Word says: "For the love of Money is the root of all kinds of evil, which while some coveted after, they have erred from the faith and pierced themselves through with many sorrows".

It is understandable that most women look out for a form of financial security from the man they intend to marry or the one they might consider, and the reasons are not far-fetched; it is just because people really don't want to suffer. However, though we may have this idea in mind, I have seen many people miss out on God's blessings for their lives by just looking at the present and what a man may represent in the present. Many ladies are carnal about some of these things and have an almost inexhaustible checklist when they meet a man. Before they know it, they have drawn up a list that speaks of perfection when they themselves are not perfect. I say this Madeleine as an introduction, because unless we take things from the root, we may not be successful in dealing with some problems.

The issue of money must be weighed very carefully. Even ladies in the church have grown to be extremely materialistic, howbeit in a subtle way, and what seems to attract women in our days are no longer the virtues of character, decency, diligence , discipline, hard work, and all other godly virtues. If a man drives a classy car and lives in a classy house, they believe it fits what God is saying to them. These are often signs of covetousness. Our master once said, "Take heed and beware of covetousness; for a man's life does not consist of the abundance of things he has". It's quite interesting that in our days, a lot of ladies actually think the opposite of what our Master says. If a lot of ladies understand this truth, they won't have unnecessary expectations.

A lot of ladies, even in the church, have imbibed the culture of 'money-tised relationships' "money-tised weddings" and other convenient or mostly inconvenient show-offs. It is interesting that as more ladies embrace this culture, they put unnecessary burdens and pressures on men, and that's why we see a lot of men who are not getting any younger, but don't seem to see themselves getting married in the nearest future. There is a culture of a fabulous proposal, an expensive diamond ring, honey-moon in three different continents and many more. While all these things are beautiful in themselves, an unnecessary and unhealthy craving for such things pushes you to the point where it is the major determinant in choosing who to marry, and the reason why a good number of people are still single. While I am not against a good wedding if you can afford one, it is important to remember that life is in phases and men are in sizes. Madeleine, I say these things because I believe this is the root cause of money problems in marriages.

You must remember that you don't go into marriage to inherit a fortune, neither do you go into marriage for selfish reasons. You go there to help. To build. A man may not have everything today but if he is on his way somewhere, it becomes a privilege to be part of helping him achieve the greatness inside of him. This is the mind-set a godly woman should have. All these things that people see as priorities, in light of eternity, are mostly irrelevant.

Finances And The Home

With the foundation laid, let's talk about finances in the home. Madeleine, it is scriptural that the man is supposed to take care of the family and meet the needs of his family. Therefore, it is expected that a man works, earns a living and has something to give to his family and others. However, I always like to talk of cases when this is not the case. What happens when you both work and you earn more than your husband? It will interest you to know that God has a say in this case. Madeleine, please note that the baton of leadership doesn't get transferred to you just because you earn more than your husband. No. My reason for saying this is that a lot of ladies who earn more than their husbands make life hell for their husbands just because they earn more than him. Interestingly, some of them are Christians, believers. It is important for you to remember that God's order of marriage doesn't say you are an equal partner with your husband. The Bible says that he is your Lord. Many may not understand this, but the Bible says 'Your husband is your Master'. An example was given in the Bible of Sarah who called her husband 'Lord'. You are daughters of Sarah if you live like this.

It will interest you to note that the account of Sarah calling Abraham Lord which the Holy Spirit documented for us was something Sarah said in her heart. It was not lip service, she really believed in the way God instituted marriage. Your husband is your master and leader, and that's why I encourage people to marry who they believe can lead them. The fact that you have more money or opportunities doesn't give you the baton of leadership.

Many ladies do not understand how God sees marriage, and Madeleine, this is one of the causes of problems in marriage. The man is seen by God as the head of the home. Many ladies for example, believe that the man should pay all the bills in the house with his money while they keep all of theirs. Please remember that you are called to help so at least it's only right to help out if there is a need to help. The fact that you earn the money doesn't mean you have the right to spend it anyhow you like without being accountable.

Many families adopt a joint account but it's not a joint account that makes money problems go away but joint-hearts. With joint-hearts you may have different accounts but you are able to do things together. Madeleine, it's important you also have initial talks on how the pattern of the family finances will go. Some people have a pool account where the expenditure of the house is taken from, others do it in other ways. Some individuals draw up a monthly budget and try to stick to it (especially if they are accountants by profession). Please ensure you discuss it and whatever suits the both of you is what you should adopt.

Finances And Extended Family

One of the things that you must know how to handle is how your man gives money to family members. Some men were the bread-winners of their extended family before they got married, however now that you are in the equation, you must tread softly. Sometimes, we can be correct in what we are saying but wrong in how we present it. This still makes us wrong in the end. There is a prevailing culture where ladies seem to despise their mothers-in-law or other family members. This should not be said about you Madeleine. Remember, you are a new creation; the love of God dwells in you, and you now have the love nature in you. You must be different. If you notice that your husband's helping of family members does not affect the family budget, it would be wise for you to leave him or to encourage him. The only time you may speak (with wisdom) is when you notice that his immediate family, which consists of you and children when they come, seem to suffer from his generosity to his extended family. You may discuss this by introducing it subtly, so he won't see it as you trying to tell him what to do.

It is very important that you deal with this issue very carefully so that your spouse does not get the impression that you are against anyone. I have noticed that it is easier for men to listen to their spouses when they have come to learn through experience that the woman is on their side. Interestingly, it is important that a man is able to discern that you are not selfish but think of his best interest every time. This is what helps him easily take up your counsel and act on it. The moment a man discerns that a woman is selfish and self- centred in her counsel to him, he will take future counsels with a pinch of salt because he will just think she is saying whatever she is saying for her benefit alone.

Finally, transparency in financial dealings is crucial in marriage. Many ladies hide money from their husbands and while there may be reasons for this, such as being married to a spend thrift, it is important that you are open to your spouse about your earnings and your money. When a man finds out later that you were hiding money from him, it makes him lose his confidence in you and his trust for you may dwindle. In all things, the most important thing is to constantly renew your mind as this is the way to know how to deal wisely in your relationship with your man. I intend to conclude this letter by talking to you about 'Renewing Your Mind'.

Renewing Your Mind

Watch What You Say

Inasmuch as it's the responsibility of every Christian to renew their minds, it is important that I remind you of it Madeleine. You must understand that as a Christian, you are now in another kingdom and we must live by the dictates of our new kingdom. That is the only way to be a success. The greatest investment you can have is a conscious investment towards mind renewal. It will bring you to a place of happiness and peace. A woman with a mind that is not renewed is dangerous to a marriage.

There are many things that can become issues in marriage which mostly boils down to the way the people in the relationship think. We are on a path of spiritual success when we decide to make the word the final authority in our lives. This puts us in a different class from everyone else. Let me give you an example of what I am talking about. The word says to us in 1 Peter 3:9 (New Living Translation) "Don't repay evil for evil . Don't retaliate with insults when people insult you. Instead pay them back with blessing. This is what God has called you to do, and he will bless you for it". Madeleine, this is what God expects from us and it takes a renewed mind to conform to this way of living. This is meant to be your Christian philosophy, the way you see life. Imagine how strange it will be if you decide to act this word out. People will not understand you, and you will be an object of pride and joy to your husband. Babes in Christ are the ones who talk anyhow; they are ready to rail at anyone who seems to offend them. My daughter Madeleine, there is a higher way to live. I am sure you have met some of these immature Christians, the ladies that I am trying to describe; they can curse for a living and they would even go further to brag about the fact that they are specially equipped to use their mouths in this way.

Please remember that renewal of mind is a process, not an instant thing. It is not something you pray about, making utterances like "Oh Lord, please renew my mind in Jesus name". Renewal of heart is never instant, it is a process and it is your responsibility not God's. You can't pray your way into a renewed mind, you can only decide to live out the word of God that you see. You can decide to plant the word of God in your heart and act upon it.

The reason why I write on renewal of heart and gave the example of the way ladies speak is because women can be very emotional. They are moved by words, controlled by words and they express themselves by words. However, God will not have us express the condition of how we feel if it will not be beneficial to the other person. The scripture says that our words are to be seasoned with salt and engraced, so that our words will edify the hearers. Therefore words that don't edify, encourage and inspire should not be known with you Madeleine.

There are some people who everyone knows for using words to spoil or condemn everything. Nothing can receive a pass mark around them. They 'bad-mouth' everything, everyone and every situation; please don't be like that. As a woman, wisdom to know that words have power and having the ability to use them wisely is the difference between a wise and a foolish woman. Even the word says that a good word makes the heart glad and it is an ambassador of healing. Madeleine, you must act out your faith by speaking faith-filled words. A lot of ladies know how to describe bad situations that may be happening in their homes, however God expects us to use our words to change what we may be experiencing.

We must speak out positively concerning the changes we want to see in our spouses. Sometimes when people pray to God concerning their spouses, all they do is just have a complaining monologue. This does not change anything. However, a better way to go about this is by thanking God for what the word says about the head of the house. Instead of praying and saying things like *"God this man will never change, he is always doing what I tell him not to do and making bad decisions"* why not change it to *"Father , I want to thank you because my husband is filled with the wisdom of God. He makes the right decisions, and I thank you because he is growing in love and in the revelation of you"*. This is a better way to pray. Instead of speaking the negative, speak words of faith that will cause you to come out of your prayer closet faith-filled based on the words you just spoke.

Understanding Right Timing

In relation to your spouse, you must understand the power of right timing, even in communication. Proverbs 15:23 says "It is wonderful to say the right things at the right time". A lot of ladies have the right thing to say but they don't know when to say it. This, most times, can get them frustrated because their spouse didn't receive what they said or shows no desire to listen to them. In understanding your man, you must understand timing. I always tell ladies never to bring up other issues when their husbands are discussing their passions. For example, a man may be talking to you about how he passionately delivered a speech at his work place, or he may be a lover of football and he is watching a match; that is not the time to discuss an important issue with him. You will end up sounding like an enemy to him. At that moment, he just wants you to listen to him and then say things like 'well done' 'I am proud of you' or 'That's my husband'. If he is watching a football game, that is not the time to talk about the family budget or the need to change the children's school. At that time, you become the best person in the world if you get him a chilled drink and maybe sit down with him and engage him in his passion.

Prayerfully Find A Mentor
As you keep planting the word, one advice I will give you is to ensure that you have a mentor. Who is a mentor? I like to describe a mentor as a 'Mental instructor', a person that aids and supports you in your growth process. The beautiful thing about having a mentor is that it saves you from making some mistakes that you would normally have made. No one is all-knowing except God, so it is important you have a mentor who can furnish you with truths that will strengthen you. The word says in Proverbs 15:7 "the lips of the wise give good advice", and we are also told in Proverbs 15:22 that "plans go wrong for lack of advice, many advisers brings success". However, I believe that you should prayerfully select your mentor because one good mentor could be more informative than a college education and more valuable than a decade's income.

Watch The Friends You Keep
It's also important that you watch the kind of friends you keep. A lot of people keep friends that lead them to destruction. One of the things friends do is that they consciously or unconsciously influence us. Madeleine my dear, even the scripture tells us that "evil communication corrupts good manners". This shows that wrong friends can cause havoc because they are sometimes the source of wrong counsel and behaviour. It is important that you keep friends that believe in the things you believe in, who fear and love the Lord and continually make His word the Lord of their lives. There are many examples of people who got the wrong counsel that cost them a lot. The son of Solomon who became king is an example; he got wrong counsel from his peers and this led to the division of Israel. Wrong counsel can divide a home. Always remember this.

Madeleine, I have spoken to you from my heart, and I have told you those things I believe you need to thrive in relationship and marriage. I definitely can't end this heart-warming letter without praying for you because it's my desire that you are a worthy wife to your husband. Proverbs 14:3 says "A worthy wife is a crown for her husband, but a disgraceful woman is like cancer in his bones". Inasmuch as God has ordained the woman to be a helper, if she doesn't understand how to function she can be a cancer to the man's destiny, causing harm and destruction, but I believe better things concerning you my dear Madeleine.

Prayer For Madeleine

This is why I bow my knees to the Father, the creator of everything in heaven and on earth, and pray that from his glorious unlimited resources, he will empower you with inner strength through His Spirit. I pray that Christ will make his home in your hearts as you trust him, and that your roots will grow down into God's love and keep you strong. May you have the power to understand as all God's people should, how wide, how long, how high, and how deep his love is. I pray that you experience the love of Christ though it is too great to be fully comprehended. I also pray you will be made complete with all the fullness of life and power that comes from God.

This is my prayer for you dear Madeleine, and I would ask that you also pray them for yourself as you embark on this journey. Finally, because I believe that to succeed in marriage, wisdom is needed, as Proverbs 14:1 says, "A wise woman builds her own home but a foolish woman tears it down with her own hands", therefore, you will need wisdom to be able to deal wisely in your position as a 'suitable helper'. Thus, I pray that the Lord grants you the spirit of wisdom and revelation in the knowledge of Him, that your eyes of understanding are enlightened to know the hope of his calling. I pray you are filled with the knowledge of God's will in all wisdom and spiritual understanding in Jesus name.

My daughter, hearken to all that is written in this letter for if you do, happy and thankful will you be. I will always love you my daughter Madeleine.

About The Author

Pastor Adedayo Babalola is the Pastor of Grace Reigns Ministry in London, United Kingdom. He has been called by God to share the message of God's grace, love and power with the world using Christ-Centred teachings to raise disciples. He has an itinerant ministry and loves to share Kingdom truths around the world. He is married to Oyenike Babalola, a gospel minister in songs and they have two lovely kids, Kharis-Krater and Kharriss-ah Zoe-Esther.

Contact The Author

To get in touch with Pastor Dayo or to invite him to
speak at your church, conference, youth/singles or
marriage seminar, please send an email to
pastordayo@grace-reigns.org or call 447983890752

www.ingramcontent.com/pod-product-compliance
Lightning Source LLC
Chambersburg PA
CBHW021145020426
42331CB00005B/903